THE BLACK DAY BOOK

DAILY TRAGIC BRIEFS

THE BLACK DAY BOOK

DAILY TRAGIC BRIEFS

PENGUIN

PENGUIN BOOKS

Published by the Penguin Group
Penguin Group (Australia)
250 Camberwell Road, Camberwell, Victoria 3124, Australia
(a division of Pearson Australia Group Pty Ltd)
Penguin Group (USA) Inc.
375 Hudson Street, New York, New York 10014, USA
Penguin Group (Canada)
90 Eglinton Avenue East, Suite 700, Toronto ON M4P 2Y3, Canada
(a division of Pearson Penguin Canada Inc.)
Penguin Books Ltd
80 Strand, London WC2R 0RL, England
Penguin Ireland
25 St Stephen's Green, Dublin 2, Ireland
(a division of Penguin Books Ltd)
Penguin Books India Pvt Ltd
11 Community Centre, Panchsheel Park, New Delhi – 110 017, India
Penguin Group (NZ)
Cnr Airborne and Rosedale Roads, Albany, Auckland, New Zealand
(a division of Pearson New Zealand Ltd)
Penguin Books (South Africa) (Pty) Ltd
24 Sturdee Avenue, Rosebank, Johannesburg 2196, South Africa

Penguin Books Ltd, Registered Offices: 80 Strand, London, WC2R 0RL, England

First published by Penguin Group (Australia), a division of Pearson Australia Group Pty Ltd, 2005

10 9 8 7 6 5 4 3 2

Text copyright © Penguin Group (Australia) 2005
Photography copyright © Getty Images

The moral right of the author has been asserted

Design by Adrian Saunders © Penguin Group (Australia)
Cover photograph by APL/Corbis
Printed in China by Everbest Printing Co. Ltd.
ISBN 0143004387

www.penguin.com.au

To my parents, Fran and Taggart Briefs, who were kind enough to wrap me in a blanket before they left me on the steps of the orphanage, twice.

THE BLACK DAY BOOK

Any day can be a black day.

These are days when you know you're a
mere speck on the face of the earth,

when you are no longer able to delude
yourself that there is a point to it all.

Life is a slog, and some days are beyond endurance.

When you're stuck in traffic,

the elements conspire against you,

your flight is cancelled.

You need to decide if you will let
the world push you around,

or if you will fight back.

On black days the world is against you.

It's right that you feel paranoid.

The panic rises,

frantically, you search for comfort
in all the wrong places,

you feel abandoned in a scorching desert

and dread lurks over your shoulder.

You can feel yourself plummeting
to the bottom of a deep pit.

Misery overwhelms you

and you wish you could just disappear
off the face of the earth

or crawl into a cave,

where no one can find you

and you can try to forget yourself.

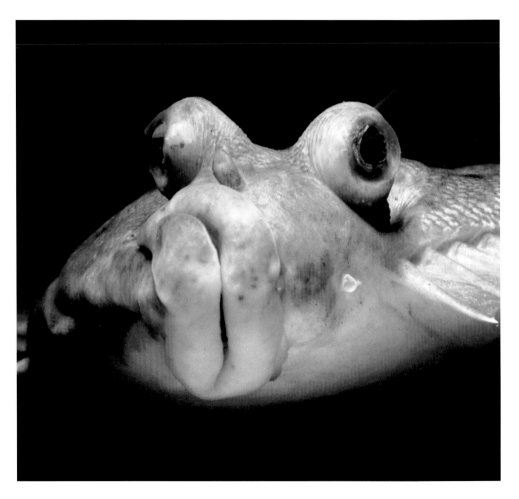

On black days nothing goes according to plan.

You can't find anything to wear,

your hair's a disaster,

you get lost,

or suffer public humiliation.

Friends and relatives turn on you,

you walk around all day with your fly unzipped,

or you're mistaken for a criminal.

You feel pushed to the edge.

Your job is a mindless grind,

everyone wants a piece of you.

You're surrounded by fools,

backed into a corner,

with no escape in sight.

You might have severe acne,

fetid breath,

rotten teeth,

putrid gas,

a strange growth,

or a face only a mother could love.

You know the world is out to get you.

So what should you do?

Nothing.

What's the point?

Things rarely get better.

It's best to just stop trying,

and surrender to the forces of the cosmos.

Just grimace and bear it.

It's important to realise you *are* alone,

responsible for your own survival,

with only your wits to rely on.

Go after what *you* want,

don't let anyone get in your way.

If someone interferes, tell them where to go.

Don't let yourself become one of those gentle
souls who wants to save the world.

Is it really worth saving?

What with pollution

and the hole in the ozone layer,

global warming,

overpopulation,

the threat of terrorism,

war,

karaoke,

and aging rock stars who just won't quit.

But worst of all there's love.

Which inevitably leads to heartbreak,

hate-mail,

emotional baggage,

paranoia,

sleeping alone,

insecurity,

loneliness

and despair.

So how can you avoid the nauseating feeling that you're sliding into a pool of squalid slime?

It's simple.

Avoid people. They're only going to hurt you.

Lose your ambition. It won't get you anywhere.

Remember that you are *always* right, and
don't let anyone tell you otherwise.

Never say you're sorry.

Don't worry about other people. They need to grow up and look after themselves.

Make scary faces at small children.

Sleep a lot – it kills time.

Stop worrying about your personal appearance,

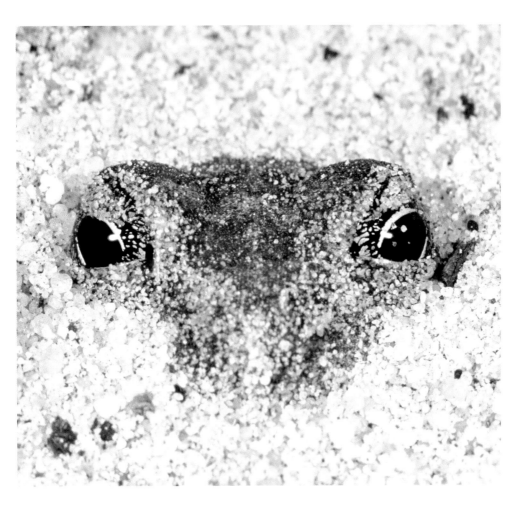

nobody notices you anyway.

Avoid positive people,

they're just deluding themselves.

Why worry about consequences?

If you're lucky, today might be your last.

Sit back and watch life pass you by.

What are you really going to miss?

Just another black day.